THE BRITISH SAILOR OF THE FIRST WORLD WAR

Quintin Colville

First published in Great Britain in 2015 by
Shire Publications, part of Bloomsbury Publishing Plc.
PO Box 883, Oxford, OX1 9PL, UK
1385 Broadway, 5th Floor, New York, NY 10018, USA
Email: shire@shirebooks.co.uk   www.shirebooks.co.uk

A CIP catalogue record for this book is available from the
British Library.

Shire Library no. 816 • ISBN-13: 978 0 74781 440 5
PDF eBook ISBN: 978 1 78442 072 7
ePub ISBN: 978 1 78442 071 0

Quintin Colville has asserted his right under the
Copyright, Designs and Patents Act, 1988, to be identified
as the author of this book.

Typeset in Garamond Pro and Gill Sans.
Printed in China through World Print Ltd.

17 18 19 20 21   11 10 9 8 7 6 5 4 3 2

COVER IMAGE
Cover design by Peter Ashley. Front cover: Detail from
the cover of *With Beatty off Jutland* by Percy F. Westerman
(collection of Peter Ashley). Back cover: Detail from 'C' in
Wills's Signalling cigarette card series (collection of Peter
Ashley).

TITLE PAGE IMAGE
Boy Seaman John Travers Cornwell, who was
posthumously awarded the Victoria Cross for his courage
in action on board HMS *Chester* at the Battle of Jutland, oil
on canvas by Ambrose McEvoy. (BHC2635: on loan from
Mrs Mona McEvoy)

CONTENTS PAGE IMAGE
Lower-deck sailors from HMS *Kent* striking a warlike pose,
c. 1914. (WHR/2/45)

ACKNOWLEDGEMENTS
The author is profoundly grateful to trail-blazing social
historians of the First World War Royal Navy such as Max
Arthur, Peter Hart, Brian Lavery, Peter Liddle, Nigel
Steel and Julian Thompson; to Andrew Lambert, Marcus
Faulkner, Mark Connelly and Laura Rowe; to friends
and colleagues at the National Maritime Museum; and to
Hannah, Douglas and Clara.

IMAGE ACKNOWLEDGEMENTS
This book is published in association with Royal Museums
Greenwich, the group name for the National Maritime
Museum, Royal Observatory Greenwich, Queen's House
and *Cutty Sark*.

www.rmg.co.uk

Images in this publication may be ordered from the Picture
Library, National Maritime Museum, Greenwich, London,
SE10 9NF or online at http://images.rmg.co.uk. The
archive reference numbers can be found in brackets at the
end of each caption.

All images © National Maritime Museum, Greenwich,
London, unless otherwise stated.

For images MNT0018 and WHR/2/45, the Museum
regrets that enquiries have not been able to identify the
copyright holder and would welcome any information
that would help it to update its records. Please contact the
Picture Library.

Shire Publications is supporting the Woodland Trust, the UK's leading woodland conservation charity, by funding the dedication of trees.

CONTENTS

INTRODUCTION

I F YOU HAD been observing the Royal Navy's ships in the opening days of the First World War you might have witnessed a curious sight. Whether at a British anchorage, or around the world from Gibraltar to Bermuda, some of the first casualties of the conflict were pianos. Already battered by rowdy evenings in the mess, and with hammers sticky from spilled beer, they were removed from gunrooms and wardrooms and either landed or unceremoniously pitched over the side. With them went assorted furniture and woodwork, comfortably domestic fittings and fixtures being considered a fire hazard if a ship was hit in combat, and also suddenly seeming rather out of keeping with the momentous news of war. This is not to say that the Navy roughed it in the years that followed. Most flag officers continued to boast day and dining cabins stocked with mahogany and silver. But these Spartan preparations reflected the reality that, after a century of relatively untroubled British sea power, the Royal Navy was facing a new European struggle and a stern test of its mettle.

Accounts and commemorations of the conflict are understandably dominated by the appalling slaughter on the Western Front. The army's loss of life has a horrifying arithmetic that the war at sea cannot match. The cultural outpouring that began with the war poets and continues to this day through novels, films and documentaries has also familiarised us with the stock characters of trench warfare:

the stoical Tommy; the well-bred young lieutenant, revolver in hand; and the well-fed general enjoying the comforts of a château far behind the lines. For all their partiality and inaccuracy, these caricatures at least give us a point of entry to the experiences of the land war. The case of the Navy is quite different. Public memory of the hundreds of thousands of men and women who served within its ranks is, by comparison, blurred and vague. Who they were, what they did, and what contribution they made, are questions that most would find hard to answer.

The aim of this book is to bring these Royal Naval lives into sharper focus. It cannot attempt to explore the immensely important role played by merchant mariners, or indeed by non-British sailors from around the world. The range of naval contexts that this involves remains extraordinarily diverse – from the mighty steel battleships that clashed at Jutland in 1916, to shallow-draft gunboats patrolling the inland waterways of what is now Iraq during the Mesopotamia campaign. What follows is also careful to show that the naval war did not simply take place on the waves. Although largely untried weapons at the beginning of the conflict, Royal Navy submarines soon proved their value, growing rapidly in

Masters of the Seas, oil on canvas by W. L. Wyllie. The leading battleship, HMS *Audacious*, had already been sunk when this painting was exhibited at the Royal Academy in 1915. (BHC4167)

Crew of the battleship *Queen Elizabeth* assembled for a visit by the Bishop of London in July 1916. (N16562: Howe Collection)

size, seaworthiness and endurance. Even the sky was a naval battleground. For Royal Naval Air Service pilots, naval war was waged at the limits of technology and with tactics and equipment that evolved with dizzying speed. Moreover, tens of thousands of sailors fought ashore as part of the Royal Naval Division: from Belgium in 1914 to Gallipoli in 1915, and from there to the killing fields of France.

The maritime struggle that involved this vast and varied cast of characters was truly global, raging from the North Sea to South America, and from Africa to China. The stakes could not have been higher. Britain's war effort depended on food and raw materials from overseas – crucial supplies that could only arrive by ship. Without sea power, rations and reinforcements could not have reached the men in the trenches, and the hundreds of thousands who fought

Royal Naval
Air Service
flying boat,
watercolour
by W. L. Wyllie,
1916. (PAF1860)

V Beach,
Cape Helles,
25 April 1915,
watercolour
depicting
the terrible
casualties
suffered during
the Gallipoli
landings, by W. L.
Wyllie, c. 1915.
(PAE0974)

alongside them from India, Australia, New Zealand, the Caribbean, Africa and Canada would never have arrived at all. From the first day of the war the German navy threatened these lifelines, and the men and women who defended them deserve a prominent place within the contemplation and commemoration of these centenary years.

1914: THE ROYAL NAVY AND ITS SAILORS

THE ROYAL NAVY was a vast and intricate tool designed to further British interests in peace and war. At the same time, it was home to the men who worked, ate, slept and took their recreation within the environments it created. The living conditions that the Navy offered were as varied as the institutional tasks it faced. Sailors in the tropics sweated in airless messes with condensation dripping from the cork-lined deckheads, while their comrades in a North Atlantic gale froze in sodden clothing with a foot of icy seawater surging back and forth beneath their hammocks. Equally, the punctilious routines of a stately battleship were quite different from the more casual atmosphere of a destroyer or submarine. Even on board the same vessel, every gradation of rank and role – from boy seaman to admiral – represented a separate microcosm of identity, behaviour and responsibility.

However, notwithstanding this complexity, some broad generalisations can be made about the Royal Navy's personnel. The first is that this was an organisation profoundly shaped by the class divisions of wider British society. From the later Victorian era to the middle of the twentieth century and beyond, the great majority of naval officers were the sons of upper-middle-class civil servants, doctors, lawyers, clergy, bankers and businessmen. To their parents, a career in the 'senior service' promised some financial security, a clearly defined ladder of promotion, and above all membership of a solidly respectable and gentlemanly profession. Moreover, it

A torpedo slung from a hoist on board the cruiser *Aurora*, 1915. (N22862: Captain Gunn Collection)

A photograph framed with embroidered silk showing Charles Herridge, a lower-deck sailor, with his wife and two daughters, c. 1914. (ZBA0021)

was a commonly held view of the time that only boys from this end of the social spectrum were likely to possess the discipline, self-control and command ability that the Navy required in its leaders. These realities were laid bare in the training the Navy provided for its youthful officer material. Opened in 1905, and built in splendour on the heights above Dartmouth, Britannia Royal Naval College was essentially a naval public school, charging fees that no working-class family could possibly afford.

The backgrounds of the fleet's lower-deck sailors – known as ratings – bore little resemblance to this picture. Many came from the ranks of the urban working class. Others were from farm-labouring families, while a significant minority were orphans and abandoned children recruited directly from quasi-naval training ships or shore schools such as the Watts Naval School, and the Royal Hospital School, Greenwich. Until the early twentieth century, these boy recruits were typically sent to one of the Navy's training hulks before they joined the fleet. Five remained in service in around 1900: HMS *St Vincent* at Portsmouth, HMS *Boscawen* at Portland, HMS *Impregnable* at Devonport, HMS *Caledonia* at Queensferry, and HMS *Ganges* at Falmouth. These antiquated ships of the line were, however, ill equipped to deal with the accelerating flow of trainees prompted by naval competition with Germany, so the Admiralty constructed two new shore-based training establishments.

The first was located in Portsmouth, and the second, larger facility – built between 1903 and 1906 – was situated in coastal countryside near Ipswich, later inheriting the name HMS *Ganges* from its floating predecessor. Boys began their training at these establishments at fifteen, and remained there for approximately one year. The bleak parade ground and single-storey dormitory blocks of *Ganges* were a far cry from the landscaped parkland of Dartmouth, and took their inspiration from reformatories founded during the Victorian era for destitute or delinquent children. Far from reprobates,

The façade and main entrance of Britannia Royal Naval College, Dartmouth, early twentieth century. (N29468)

Boy trainees manning the mast on the parade ground of HMS *Ganges*, early twentieth century. (B6715)

though, the quality of trainee ratings had increased dramatically by the start of the war. As one officer put it in 1914: 'Nothing is so astonishing as the change in the personnel of the lower deck … Twenty years ago it was far from exceptional to find men who could neither read nor write. To-day … a high standard of education prevails, and every year serves to raise it.' With industrial unions and socialist politics on the rise, not all officers displayed such unalloyed delight at the lower deck's new-found intellectual credentials. The remote and rural location of *Ganges*, miles from the troubling influence of the nearest city, was not coincidental.

In spite of the social and cultural gulf that separated them, boys on both sides of this divide must have experienced similar emotions as war clouds gathered in the summer of 1914. Postings to the fleet arrived thick and fast, followed by high-spirited train journeys to the home ports and sobering glimpses of waiting warships. For many, their allocated vessel would have been a battleship – the Navy's largest and most powerful type of warship. Heavily armed and protected by thick plates of hardened steel, they were 600 feet long and crewed on average by more than a thousand men. In order to delve a little deeper into the everyday circumstances of life afloat during the conflict, the battleship is also an ideal place to begin.

Although no newly entered cadet or boy seaman would have been permitted to use it, a hatchway at the stern of these vessels led down from the quarterdeck to the captain's accommodation. The awesome responsibilities of

Boys under training for the Royal Navy's lower deck at HMS *Ganges*, the shore establishment at Shotley, near Ipswich, early twentieth century. (L7860)

this individual were accompanied by a degree of comfort. A spacious day cabin, dining cabin, sleeping cabin and bathroom were placed at his disposal, all of which, moreover, kept pace with contemporary interior decoration. Behind the grim, grey hull were fashionably neo-Georgian white-painted walls, dado rails and chintz soft furnishings, which had themselves replaced the Victorian massed ornaments, patterned wallpapers, tassels and pot plants that had flourished a decade earlier. The layout of these compartments also created a spatial metaphor for rank. The sternmost extremity of the ship tended to be reserved for the most senior officer (the captain or, in a flagship, the admiral). The further cabins were from this apex, the more junior were the officers inhabiting them, from the commander down to the lieutenants. A glimpse into the cabin of one of the latter would have revealed a bedstead with built-in drawers, a desk and shelf with a few books, binoculars, invitations and photographs of a sweetheart, and perhaps a shotgun and a tangle of fly-fishing equipment waiting in a corner for a moment of leave.

A view of the interior of Commander Viscount Curzon's cabin on board the battleship *Queen Elizabeth*, 1916. (N16648: Howe Collection)

Engineer Lieutenant-Commander A. E. Cock lying asleep in the wardroom of HMS *Aurora*, 1915. (N22855: Captain Gunn Collection)

Often sited one deck above were the ante-room and dining room that together formed the wardroom – the communal space afforded to the ship's commissioned officers. Designed to replicate gentlemen's clubs ashore, they contained button-back sofas, easy chairs, card tables, letter racks, framed photographs of the king and queen and a much-frequented bar, behind which stewards polished glasses and served drinks. Nearby was the gunroom. This comparable but less decorous facility was for the vessel's midshipmen: boys still in their teens who had not long before been surrounded by the cricket and cream teas of cadet life. Initials were carved into the furniture, dart holes peppered the walls, and humiliating initiation rites awaited all newcomers. These unfortunates might find themselves hurled across the gunroom table or dispatched, blindfolded and on all fours, on an 'Angostura hunt' following a scent trail of pungent alcoholic droplets over an obstacle course. Navigational errors invariably resulted in a caning.

A group photograph showing the midshipmen and sub-lieutenants of HMS *Queen Elizabeth*, 1916. (N16657: Howe Collection)

Returning to the captain's quarters and then walking towards the bow would carry you through the ship's remaining ranks and the vast majority of its off-duty personnel. The first group might be warrant officers – men promoted from the lower deck but unlikely to secure further advancement, socially estranged both from the wardroom and from the lower deck they had left behind. Then came the contingent of Royal Marines whose accommodation physically separated the ship's officers from its men, a precaution established in the eighteenth century to defend shipboard authority from mutinous sailors. By this point the partition walls, cladding and ceiling panels that gave officers' cabins their homely feel would have vanished. The size and shape of the forward messes were instead dictated by the ship's internal watertight subdivisions and by the curving steel plates of the hull itself, while exposed ventilation ducts, pipes and wiring crowded the deckheads. Here and there, curtains enclosed areas for the sole use of engine-room artificers or senior ratings, such as chief petty officers and petty officers, but the bulk of the space served as open mess decks for the seamen and stokers who worked the ship.

For these men, life afloat was inescapably cheek-by-jowl. Above their heads hung 'cringle' bars from which rows of closely-packed canvas hammocks were suspended, their design little changed since the days of Nelson. With a full wartime complement, there was never enough slinging space for all, and dozens slept in passageways, workshops, even in the gun turrets. Wooden slab tables and benches were packed in rows along the sides of the vessel beneath the hammock billets, with bread lockers and racks for utensils fixed above them. Each table seated a group of men, which constituted a 'mess' – the building block of lower-deck existence, and a source of crucial friendships and loyalties. Every seaman would take it in turn to draw and prepare provisions for his messmates, with some more skilled than others at staple naval recipes such as 'schooner on the rocks'

Lower-deck sailors photographed by one of HMS *Queen Elizabeth*'s turrets, 1916. (N16724: Howe Collection)

A boxing contest on board HMS *Queen Elizabeth*, 1915–16. (N16584: Howe Collection)

(shin of beef on a bed of potatoes). Dishes were washed up in the large copper kettles then used to brew tea or cocoa. Reading or writing letters could bring some respite from the intense communality, but privacy was non-existent and the only place for personal possessions was a small wooden container issued to each man and known as a 'ditty box'. Some diversion from these unchanging surroundings came in the form of keenly contested boat-pulling and sailing regattas, boxing tournaments, the ship's band and, if shore facilities were available, football.

A Royal Navy battleship was, therefore, a workplace and living environment of enormous human complexity. The stark division between upper-middle-class officers and working-class ratings was real enough, but everyday life was rarely experienced in simple 'us' and 'them' terms.

Instead, rank, age, professional specialism and length of service ensured that this world usually functioned as a stable and finely graded hierarchy. While discipline was harsh and omnipresent, the strength of a crew did not reside in threats of punishment but in co-operation, relative consensus and a shared sense of purpose. Unrest did occur and officers frequently demonstrated an alarmist attitude to the nature of lower-deck protest. The altered social dynamics of the much-expanded wartime Navy also brought new pressures. Furthermore, the service had by no means resolved the tensions of role and status generated by warships packed with new machinery and technologies – from torpedoes to aircraft. However, as a social organism, the Royal Navy that faced German sea power in 1914 was set on deep and solid foundations.

The ship's band of HMS *Aurora* assembled on the vessel's quarterdeck, 1916. (N22735: Captain Gunn Collection)

FIGHTING A GLOBAL WAR

THE DETERIORATING INTERNATIONAL situation preceding Britain's declaration of war on 4 August was not lost on the Royal Navy's personnel. With his customary copperplate hand, Paymaster Bernard Colson's diary entry for 28 July noted that his will and insurance policy were on their way to the bank for safekeeping. The same day, but thousands of miles away on the China station, Commander Edward Jukes-Hughes of HMS *Minotaur* recorded how 'during the forenoon it became evident that there was some kind of panic.' On 1 August, Cadet Lowry was preparing a snack at Britannia Royal Naval College and had 'just mashed up a banana, covered it with Devonshire cream and sugar, when a Cadet Captain rushed into the canteen and said "Mobilise". I left it untasted and ran.' At that very moment the crew of the battle-cruiser *Invincible* in the Mediterranean was hastily readying the ship for sea amid reports of impending crisis. With the task complete, an exhausted junior officer called Hubert Dannreuther collapsed into his bunk. 'I was woken up at midnight', he recalled, 'to be told that … hostilities were to commence against Germany at once; but was so sleepy that I didn't take much notice of it and wondered if I had dreamt it this morning.' He had not. As Cadet Kenneth Edwards confided to his journal on 4 August, 'we are in it now.'

Less than a fortnight later, Lieutenant Robert Don Oliver wrote to his father from HMS *Inflexible* in a disgruntled frame of mind. 'So far', he began, 'this has been the most miserably boring effort at a war that it has ever been my misfortune to take part in.' His *ennui* was destined to be short-lived. Germany's naval commanders were only too aware of the sinews of Britain's maritime greatness: a colossal navy, a merchant fleet comprising almost half of the world's commercial shipping, and a sprawling imperial network of bases and coaling stations. However, they also correctly concluded that even a trans-oceanic superpower could not be everywhere at once and in force. Unprotected merchant vessels, isolated or outdated warships, transmitting stations and territorial outposts were vulnerable, and German surface units in Caribbean, African and Far Eastern waters were ready to exploit these weaknesses wherever they found them. Oliver's short phoney war of early August soon became a bitter and far-flung struggle that would cost the lives of many of his fellow servicemen.

The first months of the war saw powerful German warships such as the *Karlsruhe, Emden, Scharnhorst, Gneisenau, Dresden, Nürnberg, Leipzig* and *Königsberg* on the loose around the globe. By the end of October, Royal Naval warships had bottled up the *Königsberg* in an East African river delta. On 9 November, HMAS *Sydney* of the Royal Australian Navy forced the *Emden* to beach itself on the Cocos Islands in the Indian Ocean. However, the first major naval clash in distant waters had occurred on 1 November off the coast of Chile and was an unmitigated disaster for the British. The German admiral, Maximilian von Spee, commanding a modern and combat-ready squadron from his flagship *Scharnhorst*, encountered a weak and outmoded British force at the Battle of Coronel. Two British cruisers were destroyed and more than 1,600 men were lost in the Royal Navy's first significant defeat for more than a century. Back in Britain, Cadet Kenneth Edwards wrote on learning the news: 'many old friends gone, but a fine sporting action.'

The British flagship, HMS *Good Hope*, ablaze during the Battle of Coronel, watercolour by W. L. Wyllie, c. 1915. (PAF1790)

For the Admiralty no possible consolation, gentlemanly or otherwise, could be drawn from this setback, and additional warships commanded by Admiral Sturdee were immediately dispatched to the South Atlantic to redress the balance. On board one of them, HMS *Kent*, Lieutenant J. K. Whittaker recorded the everyday events of a voyage whose frequent monotony and tedium belied its deadly purpose. Taking on board provisions en route was a gala day:

> People cannot imagine what a delight to us it was to get fresh meat ... our menu consisted of salt pork and peas pudding one day, and stringy bully beef with dried peas or beans the next ... the smell of the salt pork with the porker's bristles still sticking out [was] quite enough for me.

Another source of diversion was the 'Kent Kronical', the ship's monthly magazine. The 'celebrity page' of its 1 December issue profiled the vessel's gunnery officer, listing his recreations as 'watching footer matches, breaking targets, ranging guns, shooting, knitting, marbles and ping pong'. Spoof advertisements included one for 'Pickthorn's Popular Painless Panacea', asking 'Do you suffer? Pains in the Pantry, shortness of the Canteen, Coals, Catarrh, Confinement, and that Censored Feeling.'

All such amusements came to an abrupt end on 8 December, when Sturdee's force of battle-cruisers and cruisers met von Spee's ships off the Falkland Islands. A short and brutal battle followed in which four German warships were sunk with little cost to the British. Von Spee and both his sons were among those killed. For Lieutenant Whittaker those hours left an indelible

Miniature of Graham Trounson, a seventeen-year-old midshipman killed on board HMS *Good Hope* at the Battle of Coronel, watercolour by unidentified artist signing 'MH', c. 1914. (MNT0018)

Admiral Sir Frederick Doveton Sturdee, the British commander-in-chief at the Battle of the Falkland Islands, oil on canvas by Sir Arthur Stockdale Cope, 1920. (BHC3042)

Admiral
Sturdee's
ships pursuing
the German
squadron at
the start of the
Battle of the
Falkland Islands,
watercolour
by W. L. Wyllie,
c. 1915–18.
(PAF2120)

The destruction
of SMS
Scharnhorst and
Gneisenau at
the Battle of
the Falkland
Islands, by W. L.
Wyllie, 1915–18.
(PAF0922)

British warships
rescuing German
survivors in the
aftermath of the
Battle of the
Falkland Islands,
1914. (DAN/516:
reproduced
by kind
permission of
the Dannreuther
family)

Model of SMS *Scharnhorst* made in captivity by German prisoners of war from the Battle of the Falkland Islands, 1915. (SLR1371)

impression of close-range shellfire smashing into the cruiser *Nürnberg*. His conviction that 'her decks must simply have been a shambles' was confirmed when HMS *Kent* pulled twelve survivors from the bone-chilling water. '[They] were all taken below', he continued, 'where artificial respiration was resorted to … and the look of terror on their faces when they regained consciousness was truly horrible, a sure proof of what they had suffered … under our fire.' Sylvester Pawley in HMS *Glasgow* drew another lesson from the battle:

> Action in war develops qualities for good or evil, pity or contempt, and those who before that severe test would be dismissed as weak and helpless suddenly display qualities of greatness. On the other hand men in whom you have had every confidence and are the embodiment of pluck and courage become dejected and hysterical.

Even so, the blistering realities of battle were once again exchanged for routine, albeit leavened by the Navy's distinctive traditions. On 24 December, far from home and loved ones, the crew of the *Kent* gathered greenery from a Chilean hillside to decorate the ship. Christmas Day was marked with a festive version of captain's rounds, with the ship's commanding

officer processing through each mess, where he was entertained with alcohol-laden hospitality. An element of Twelfth-Night hilarity also temporarily punctured the stern face of rank and authority. Walking behind the captain, wearing one of the second-in-command's uniform jackets, and dishing out imaginary punishments to all and sundry was one of the *Kent*'s junior stokers. Soon afterwards, a sports day proved a great success, with prizes presented by the 'Duchess of Vallemar'. Extending an established naval fondness for cross-dressing, this redoubtable lady was, in fact, a certain Lieutenant Jones 'attired in the Captain of Marines' Japanese kimono, [and] long white stockings with pink garters showing.'

The last five months of 1914 had seen the Royal Navy in action from Tsingtao (Qingdao) in China to Duala in the Cameroons – an immense human and logistical undertaking. The new year would bring fresh overseas naval challenges.

A Christmas gift of tobacco sent to members of Britain's armed forces by charitable subscription. (AAB0381)

Midshipmen and sub-lieutenants of HMS *Queen Elizabeth* in costume for an amateur theatrical performance, 1916. (N16513: Howe Collection)

HMS *Kent* pursued the sole surviving German warship from the Battle of the Falkland Islands – SMS *Dresden* – until it was cornered and scuttled in March. British gunboats fought on Lake Tanganyika while, in the Mediterranean, the Navy paid a heavy price during the Dardanelles campaign before the ill-fated Gallipoli landings. Watching from HMS *Marmora* at anchor at Gibraltar in August 1915, wireless operator Percy Hanson scanned the procession of hospital ships heading home from the Dardanelles. 'It is a most pitiable sight', he wrote, 'to see such fine lads cut up and maimed, some of them for life. Many have died during the short time their ship has been at Gibraltar.'

Nonetheless – and in spite of a multitude of exceptions – British power had already begun to concentrate the naval war in more northerly waters.

Indian troops taking part in British naval landings against German forces in China, c. 1914–15. (JOD/117)

A rating on board the battleship *Queen Elizabeth* displaying a steel plate pierced by Turkish fire during the Dardanelles campaign, 1915–16. (N16837: Howe Collection)

THE NAVY IN NORTHERN WATERS: 1914–15

WHILE THE ANGLO-GERMAN naval war cast tentacles around the globe, its focus was the North Sea and the Channel. From key bases at Wilhelmshaven, Bremerhaven and Kiel a narrow stretch of water separated the High Seas Fleet from the concentrations of British naval power at Scapa Flow, Cromarty and Rosyth in the north, and Harwich, Sheerness, Chatham and Dover in the south. It was here that the majority of the 380,000 men serving in the Royal Navy by the end of the war – whether regulars, reservists or 'hostilities only' recruits – were stationed. However, their presence within this single theatre by no means suggests a uniformity of experience. The living conditions and threats facing the crews of the Grand Fleet's battleships were quite different from the realities encountered by submariners or by sailors on board the hundreds of minesweeping craft employed to keep sea lanes and harbours open. From coastal motor boats on high-speed missions, to requisitioned trawlers hunting U-boats, to destroyers escorting liners packed with troops bound for the trenches, the context was one of extraordinarily energetic and multifaceted activity. And patrolling ceaselessly in the stormy seas between Scotland, Iceland and the coast of Norway were the blockading cruiser squadrons, preventing merchant vessels loaded with war materials and foodstuffs from reaching German ports.

These wartime exigencies did not, though, eradicate the everyday customs and duties that marked the peacetime Navy.

HMS *Hogue* sinking, with the upturned hull of HMS *Aboukir* visible in the foreground, watercolour by W. L. Wyllie, c. 1915. (PAD9942)

For instance, the lower deck of most warships continued to be a hive of private enterprise. As James Cox recalled:

> I took up haircutting … Another person would buy lemonade powder and a hundredweight of sugar off the pusser [purser], and make a couple of buckets of lemonade every night, and sell it for a penny a glass … Another person would make clothes … [and] someone else would do other people's washing.

Cartoon showing the crew of an armed fishing vessel destroying a German submarine, 1920. (CLO298:6/6)

The daily rum ration – issued diluted as 'grog' – was still more sacred. Solemnly issued with gleaming copper measures from a large wooden tub, this prized spirit also maintained its longstanding use as a shipboard currency for favours of

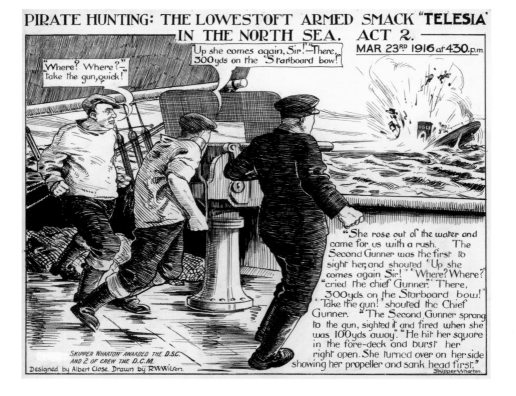

PIRATE HUNTING: THE LOWESTOFT ARMED SMACK "TELESIA" IN THE NORTH SEA. ACT 2.
MAR 23RD 1916 at 4.30 p.m.

A sailor receiving a haircut on the deck of a British warship, 1914–18. (N24247: Laforey Collection)

every kind. Other practices were loathed rather than loved. Whether in peace or war, the Navy's ships needed fuel and the task of coaling – not to mention the subsequent work of cleaning a ship carpeted with coal dust – was universally detested. One sailor described bringing 2,500 tons of coal on board ship as follows:

> Throughout the night the shovels were working and the winches rattling away … Those poor devils in the bowels of the ship were trimming the bunkers as the coal shot into them. The stokers were enshrouded with an indescribable cloud of dust, which got right into the lungs, and they had only a Davy safety lamp to guide them.

Nevertheless, the conflict threaded fear and foreboding through every activity. A mine, struck by a vessel while under way, or a torpedo fired from a hidden foe could in an instant turn a scene of tranquil normality into a hell of twisted metal and scalding steam. In October 1914 the first happened to the battleship *Audacious*, which was sunk by one of the 43,000 mines laid by the German navy during the war.

The battleship *Audacious* sinking off the Irish coast after striking a German mine in October 1914, watercolour by W. L. Wyllie, c. 1918. (PAF1831)

Still deeper shock had been caused the previous month when, in just over an hour, a lone U-boat torpedoed and sank three cruisers off the Dutch coast – the *Hogue*, *Aboukir* and *Cressy* – with the loss of 1,459 officers and men. These new weapons had an immense psychological impact, but they were not the only hazards. On 26 November 1914, the battleship *Bulwark* was ripped apart by an internal explosion, probably caused by over-heated cordite charges in one of its magazines. More than 700 men died. Watching from a nearby warship, Midshipman Williams described how

> our cutter came back with some bits, one poor fellow blown clean in half at the waist, only just his chest and head, and a lot of other bits, legs etc. all horribly cut about. All the officers were on the quarter deck looking sick as mud and I felt horribly ill … It really was a horrible sight, everything splashed with blood, just like a beef boat coming alongside, the whole bodies weren't so bad, but the bits were filthy and everyone was feeling rather rotten for the rest of the day.

The cruiser *Hermes* sinking in the Strait of Dover after being torpedoed by a German submarine in October 1914. (D47/E)

The bow of HMS *Mentor* showing the damage caused by a German torpedo during a mission in the North Sea, 1915. (N22531: Captain Gunn Collection)

Even the elements could prove fatal. Several blockading vessels foundered in heavy seas, and Petty Officer E. Phillips has left a vivid account of ferocious weather that hit the battleship *Barham* in the North Sea on 23 December 1915.

We increased speed to 23 knots and then the fun started, we shipped big green seas over the starboard side and they swept everything with them, the sea lifted the … [ship's boats] out of their crutches and stood them up against X turret … another sea hit the 6" [gun] on the upper deck starboard side … and opened the shield out like an umbrella breaking the sights and carrying away the rack for storage of projectiles … talk about a big ship for comfort, we had to sit in the mess tub and paddle in the mess for dinner.

Then there was the ever-present threat that the parting of a fog bank or the lifting of a mist might turn one of the Navy's endless North Sea patrols into a deadly clash with German surface forces. Two major encounters marked the first months of the war – the Battle of Heligoland Bight in August 1914 and the Battle of Dogger Bank in January 1915. While both were British victories, neither side was spared the horrors of modern naval warfare that these engagements placed in sharp relief. The crew of a warship shared an approximate equality of vulnerability to death and injury. However, every action station held its own specific terrors. Ratings manning guns on the upper deck and officers giving orders from the bridge were directly exposed to the blast of high explosive and the gruesome shards from shell casings that decapitated, disembowelled or dismembered anyone in their path. After the Heligoland Bight action, Commander Lennon Goldsmith remembered how the destroyer *Laurel* was hit: 'the main effect … was to blow the centre gun's crew literally to bits – almost nothing was found of them. She lurched away in a dense cloud of black smoke, with the Captain wounded by splinters of brass bridge rail.'

British destroyers coming under fire at the Battle of Heligoland Bight in August 1914, by W. L. Wyllie, c. 1914. (PAF1232)

Scene on board a British light cruiser in action at the Battle of Dogger Bank in January 1915, by W. L. Wyllie, c. 1915–18. (PAF1840)

The effect of a shell detonating within a closed compartment was, if possible, even more horrifying. A report written by a survivor from the German armoured cruiser SMS *Blücher*, sunk at Dogger Bank, provides some indication:

> All loose or insecure fittings are transformed into moving instruments of destruction. Open doors bang to and jam. Closed doors bend outward like tin plates and through it

A type of hammock used on board Royal Naval warships for wounded or injured personnel, c. 1914–18. (ZBA0556)

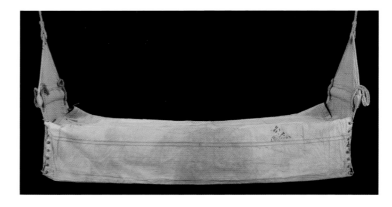

all, the bodies of men are whirled about like dead leaves in a winter blast to be battered to death against the iron walls … Everywhere blood trickled and flowed.

Men far beneath the waterline in engine rooms or magazines were spared some of this but lived with the certain knowledge that in a crisis watertight hatches, decks and companionways stood between them and the slim hope of survival. Servicemen at both ends of the conflict would have identified with F. W. Turpin's wry assessment of his chances in the bowels of HMS *Agamemnon*.

The German cruiser *Blücher* is shown here shortly before capsizing and sinking at the Battle of Dogger Bank, watercolour by W. L. Wyllie, 1916. (PAF1765)

My station in battle is … in the shell room of our after 12" guns. There it is my duty to help load … projectiles weighing nearly 1000 lbs each … to feed the gun up above. We are hideously attired in masks and with goggles, respirators and anti-gas apparatus resemble demons from the nether world …
You feel the deck reel under your feet from the terrific effect of a broadside and you realise to the full that war is a monstrous thing. I am fairly safe in my shellroom from direct fire but if anything should cause the ship to sink fairly quickly this diary would remain unfinished.

With a degree of candour not always present in contemporary accounts, an officer in HMS *Arethusa* reflected on the altered atmosphere produced by the fighting at Heligoland Bight. 'There is a marked difference', he noted,

in the feelings both of officers and men to those shown when we set out on our first adventure. Then we were light-hearted and eager. We talked about hoping to see some 'fun'. Now it is very different. I do not believe there is one officer or man who was on board … who will light-heartedly enter a second fight. Fear is undoubtedly knocking on our hearts … We will all do our job – there assuredly will be no shrinking, but I at least can not help being terribly 'nervy'. I wonder if this is a terrible confession. I sincerely hope that I will become more callous very soon, as at present I am feeling the strain, though of course I can not show it.

A candelabrum and tea caddy damaged when a German shell hit Admiral Beatty's cabin on board HMS *Lion* at the Battle of Dogger Bank. (PLT0018, PLT0745)

And behind these private and personal misgivings lay the nagging, communal anxiety that the great, knock-out, Nelsonian victory that the nation expected had yet to materialise.

Royal Naval Division

France 1916

Up Anchor!

THE NAVY'S WAR ON LAND AND IN THE AIR

FAR FROM BEING fought exclusively at sea, the naval war was marked by an extraordinary diversity of contexts, roles and skills. To begin with, it is important to note that the Navy went to war with a significant manpower surplus. As a direct result, thousands of Royal Naval and Royal Marine reservists and volunteers were formed into battalions to serve on land as infantrymen. In August 1914, this force became known as the Royal Naval Division and its casualties constituted a large proportion of the Royal Navy's overall losses. At the same time, the Navy was also at the forefront of an entirely new dimension of modern warfare: powered flight. The Royal Naval Air Service (RNAS) began the war as the world's largest naval air corps, with ninety-three seaplanes and aeroplanes, seven airships, and approaching one thousand personnel. By early 1918, when the RNAS became part of the newly formed Royal Air Force, this had grown to 2,949 aeroplanes, seaplanes and flying boats, about 130 airships and more than 55,000 pilots and ground staff. Weapons whose realistic application had only been demonstrated a few years before fighting broke out, rapidly developed tactical and strategic roles that remain with us today.

In its first few months, the Royal Naval Division was not as formidable as it later became. Hastily assembled, its equipment – including outmoded rifles – certainly left much to be desired. As Leonard Sellers remembered: 'We were served out with the old leather equipment as was used in the

Entitled 'Up Anchor!', this is a Royal Naval Division postcard from the Western Front, 1916. (AAB0510)

An altar cross made from a German bullet and cartridge case and used by a Royal Naval Division chaplain on the Western Front, 1914–16. (AAA0081)

Boer War. Needless to say, it was in a shocking state … hard as iron, mildewed.' Moreover, the idea of serving ashore did not meet with universal delight. One ordinary seaman, John Bentham, recalled that 'The commodore … informed us that all our hopes of going to sea were dead … This was a real blow and everyone was very depressed. We even held a solemn mock funeral in which our officers took part and a copy of the Admiralty Seamanship Manual was lowered into the Thames.' Training was sometimes rather perfunctory. In the words of Leonard Sellers again: 'None of the officers had the slightest idea of army drill and it was quite a common sight to see company commanders reading out commands [from the handbook]'. Casualties were unsurprisingly high when battalions were deployed to Flanders in late August 1914, encountering the chaotic and fast-moving struggle around Antwerp. The German advance also forced 1,500 sailors to withdraw into the neutral Netherlands, where they were interned for the rest of the war.

By early 1915, British attention was increasingly focused on the Dardanelles. Then controlled by the hostile Ottoman Empire, this narrow sea route linked the Mediterranean to the Black Sea ports of Russia, a British ally. In April, naval forces supported a vast seaborne invasion of the Gallipoli peninsula, which forms the north shore of the Dardanelles. The Royal Naval Division took part, alongside troops from Australia, New Zealand, India, Newfoundland and France. On the first day of the landings – 25 April 1915 – Sub-Lieutenant Arthur Tisdall of the division's Anson Battalion was awarded the Victoria Cross for rescuing soldiers trapped between the troopship *River Clyde* and the beachhead. Kenneth Edwards

watched the scene from on board the battleship *Lord Nelson*: 'the *River Clyde* ... appeared thro' the smoke, and half a dozen picket boats towing cutters full of troops. They were met by a fearful fire from pompoms, Maxims and rifles which had been most cleverly and efficiently shielded, and the men were mown down in hundreds.' This ferocious reception was matched by the months of bloody fighting that followed and the campaign was abandoned in January 1916. The Royal Naval Division alone had lost 7,198 men killed or wounded.

Only a few months later, the division was transported to Marseilles en route to the Western Front. The naval surgeon, Geoffrey Sparrow, remembered their arrival, and the 'miles of vineyards and green fields with pink-tinted hills in the distance ... every station was lined with cheering crowds, who welcomed us to France and showered gifts of food and wine

upon us.' What awaited them, though, was a procession of horror, from the Battle of the Somme in 1916 to Passchendaele in 1917 and the final British offensive of 1918. Sparrow remembered how each man soon became 'inured to the gruesome sight of a shattered form and a blood-stained firestep, but the haunting thought sooner or later enters his brain that some day his blood will stain the firestep, his mangled body block the trench, his wife be a widow, and his children fatherless.' Demobilised in 1919, and frankly astonished at his own survival, Hubert Trotman made his way back to his family home near Didcot:

Portrait photograph of Surgeon Lieutenant Charles Edward Leake, who served on the Western Front with the Royal Naval Division, 1914–18. (C7125)

My sister was there to meet me and my mother. We kissed and jabbered away. Then my mother went to fetch my dear father. She came rushing out of the bedroom. 'Hubert, your dad has gone to pieces, he's just laying there like a log, he just passed out'. He had heard my voice and was totally overcome. With all the Royal Naval Division casualties I don't think he ever expected me to return.

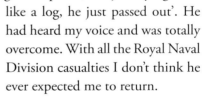

Military Cross with bar awarded to Surgeon Lieutenant Charles Edward Leake in 1918 for tending to wounded servicemen under fire. (MED1664)

Whether fighting at Gallipoli or mired in the trenches of northern France, the men of the Royal Naval Division would have noticed the increasing importance and visibility of air power. They would also have known that many of the fragile craft fighting above them were flown by their naval comrades-in-arms.

Uniform dress tunic of a Royal Naval Division surgeon, 1917. (UNI0991)

Kindred spirit may not, however, have stretched all that far. With a reputation for fierce independent-mindedness, the RNAS was both professionally and socially removed from everyday naval life, while at the same time absorbed in its own frantic cycle of technological development. The RNAS training manual from November 1914 captures something of this pioneering sensibility: 'It must be borne in mind that the whole subject is at present in a very experimental stage and that it is impossible in many cases to lay down hard and fast rules of procedure.'

As this might suggest, for would-be naval pilots the period of training was challenging, to say the least. To be

A Royal Naval Air Service Short Type-184 seaplane carrying a pair of anti-submarine bombs, watercolour by W. L. Wyllie, 1915–18. (PAE1286)

Steering wheel from a German Zeppelin destroyed by British forces, c. 1914. (REL0702)

sure, the machines used for this purpose had few of the complexities of modern aircraft. With a top speed of around 50 knots (57 mph), their dashboards carried only a compass, air-speed indicator, altimeter, side-slip bubble and sometimes a temperature gauge. Nor was the training any more sophisticated. Harold Rosher described the teaching methods applied by his instructor: 'in the air, he bawls in your ear, "Now when you push your hand forward, you go down, see! ... and when you pull it back you go up" ... Then he says "If you do so and so, you will break your neck".' This relative simplicity was, however, outweighed by the extreme unreliability of the equipment. The diary of Squadron Leader Bartlett from 25 March 1917 records how a fellow pilot, 'was seen to enter a cloud ... at about 2000 feet and a moment later reappeared side-slipping badly; the large single strut apparently collapsed under the strain ... [the wings] were wrenched off and the fuselage came down whistling like a bomb.' Engine failure was particularly common. Rosher described ditching in the sea at Dunkirk after one such occurrence: 'I hit the water with a bit of a biff ... I pulled myself together, and says I to myself ...

A Royal Naval Air Service Deperdussin monoplane on its launching platform on board the cruiser *Aurora*, 1915. (N22556: Captain Gunn Collection)

"Harold, my boy, if you don't keep your head and get out of this damn quick, you'll drown for a cert like a rat in a trap".'

The wartime roles demanded of RNAS aircrew were varied, including: anti-Zeppelin patrols; the bombing of Zeppelin sheds, U-boat bases and docks; gunnery spotting; the use of torpedoes; and, of course, aerial combat against enemy aircraft. In addition, extensive use was made of airships and reconnaissance balloons. Air stations mushroomed across the theatres of conflict, while at sea warships frequently carried seaplanes (which were lowered into the water for take-off), while others had platforms from which aircraft could be launched.

The experience of air warfare itself emerges from all accounts as shatteringly intense. Bartlett described a bombing raid over Bruges on 3 June 1917 as follows:

> Every battery was now concentrated on us and we were continually bracketed fore and aft, on both flanks, above and below, and turn, twist, zoom and sideslip as I did, I could not shake them off and thought every next salvo would get us. We were surrounded by the acrid smoke of near misses and ... our old DH4 was tossed bodily by the blast.

British aircraft raiding German positions in France or Belgium, watercolour by W. L. Wyllie, 1916–18. (PAF1551)

As if that was not sufficient, a German fighter plane then attacked and 'a bullet whizzed about an inch in front of my face shattering to fragments my starting mag. switch on the dashboard.' Harold Rosher also recorded the experience of coming under anti-aircraft fire, or 'Archie' as it was known. 'My eyes must have been sticking out of my head like a shrimp's ... I was gasping for breath and crouching down in the fuselage.' In typically clipped fashion, the highly decorated pilot Albert Enstone wrote up one dogfight over Zeebrugge on 12 May

1917 in his log: 'Attacked by Huns … Got one certain, then gun jambed [sic] and I was chased by two and badly shot up. 36 holes in machine; centre section, wings etc. had to be replaced.'

Such experiences by definition gave naval pilots a unique perspective on the war. Nevertheless, they were also connected to broader realities felt by everyone who fought. Accounts from sea, land and air stress that life yawed between the terror and exhilaration of battle, and an everyday world of routine duties and recreations. Bartlett, for instance, followed a morning bombing raid over Ostend in November 1916 with some leisurely tourism in northern France: 'After lunch … I walked into Bergues, a highly interesting old town, cathedral with fine stained glass … [and] some picturesque old buildings.' In similar vein, Geoffrey Sparrow wrote of Royal Naval Division sailors that 'They ruthlessly kill Boches, and … [come] face to face with almost certain death, but still on the following night … [are] shrieking with laughter over the ridiculous antics of their prime favourite, Charlie Chaplin.' And, for all involved, the shattering impact of casualties within tight-knit groups of friends and comrades had to be muffled and suppressed. One pilot, Robert Compston, outlined what must have been a common coping mechanism: 'By virtue of living on the surface, by turning our faces away and refusing to acknowledge death … we were able to sit down and enjoy a good breakfast.' On 28 July 1917, Albert Enstone witnessed the final moments of his friend Arnold Chadwick. The matter-of-fact entry in his flying log suggests that men did their best to place such incidents beyond the reach of emotion: 'Saw Chadwick's machine crash into sea off La Panne & break to pieces. – Chad drowned.' The psychological demands of the Great War can barely be imagined.

Portrait photograph from around 1918 of Captain Albert James Enstone, who served in the Royal Naval Air Service until it became part of the Royal Air Force in 1918. (MSS/72/094.2)

THE NAVY'S WAR BENEATH THE WAVES

THE PRE-WAR ROYAL NAVY stood at the forefront of many technological realms, among them the world of undersea warfare. Its first submarine had been launched in 1901, followed by a succession of new and improved designs generally intended for coastal defence roles. By the start of hostilities, more than sixty boats were in full commission including the latest D- and E-class vessels, whose diesel engines and improved habitability allowed for lengthier missions. The 168 officers and 1,250 ratings who manned them in August 1914 had little by way of precedent to guide their wartime activities. Nonetheless, they rapidly proved themselves effective and often spearheaded the Navy's operations in the North Sea, the Dardanelles, the Adriatic and the Baltic. In the process, the submarine fleet grew dramatically, and was ultimately credited with sinking fifty-four enemy warships (including nineteen German U-boats), and 274 transports and supply ships. The cost in men and materiel was also high: dozens of British submarines were lost and approximately 1,200 sailors were killed. In fact, it has been calculated that one third of those who joined the submarine service paid for the decision with their lives – the worst casualty statistics for any branch of the seagoing fleet.

The Navy's submariners resembled the Royal Naval Air Service in being, to some extent, a breed apart. To begin with, every man among them was a volunteer. As an inducement for accepting the hazards of this life, they were paid significantly more than their peers in surface ships, but there was also an

Officers posing on board a British submarine, c. 1915. (MS/79/105)

The Royal Naval submarine *D3* undergoing wartime repairs, 1914–18. (N22626: Captain Gunn Collection)

informality and camaraderie among submariners that many found appealing. Unlike the one thousand or more personnel on board a capital ship, submarine crews typically ranged from twenty to sixty men. Furthermore, the limited turnover within these crews welded them into tight fighting units, and blurred the boundaries of rank and class in ways that would have been unthinkable in a large warship. These realities were heightened by sheer physical confinement. With machinery, pipes and valves sprouting from every surface, space could not be spared for the elaborately zoned accommodation and hierarchical demarcations of a battleship. There were no cooks, no stewards to serve evening drinks, and no Royal Marine servants to sponge and press uniform jackets. At best a few hot plates and a small electric oven sufficed to heat up tinned provisions when circumstances permitted. The clothes that men wore at the start of a patrol were glued to their bodies with dirt, sweat and oil when they returned a fortnight later; and while the captain had a bunk, the remainder of the crew slept wherever they could.

Even without the presence of an enemy, conditions on board these boats were astonishingly gruelling. It was not coincidental that applicants were subjected to a particularly

The British submarines *E26*, *E53* and *D1* alongside the depot ship *Maidstone* at Harwich, 1916. (N24165: Laforey Collection)

thorough medical. As the Admiralty's understated instructions put it: 'Men selected for the Submarine Service are to be of good physique and capable of sustaining a considerable amount of bodily strain.' Clothing was permanently damp from condensation, after a few days the smell on board was described by one officer as 'most revolting', and high levels of carbon dioxide caused nausea, headaches and lassitude – often dangerously degrading decision-making faculties. Exhaustion compounded these problems, with most men surviving on four hours of sleep a day.

The potential for serious illness and injury was ever-present. Concussions and broken bones were the common upshot when boats hit foul weather, suffered buoyancy fluctuations or ran aground. If seawater reached a submarine's batteries, the resulting clouds of chlorine gas could asphyxiate the crew and there was no shortage of flammable chemicals that might cause fires or explosions.

Distinguished Service Order with two bars awarded to Max Kennedy Horton while a submarine commander between 1914 and 1920. (MED2549)

Submarines did not carry doctors and sailors fell back on basic first aid skills to treat their wounded comrades. One lieutenant recounted his experiences after receiving severe burns during a lengthy mission:

> my feet and legs … were a horrid sight – covered with huge blisters like Portuguese men-of-war … I now suffer torture when I have to use my feet. As a matter of fact I sort of swing along from pipe to pipe and beam to beam … Our medical book is of no help for it only gives directions for a couple of days' treatment.

Officers on the conning tower of HMS *E22*. The photograph was taken shortly before *E22* was torpedoed and sunk by a German submarine in 1916. (N24167: Laforey Collection)

Termed 'nervous strain' or 'war shock', the appalling psychological pressures of undersea warfare could also bring on mental collapse – particularly among commanding officers, whose every decision could mean life or death.

HMS *G13*, probably shown at the beginning or end of a North Sea patrol, by W. L. Wyllie, 1916. (PAF1850)

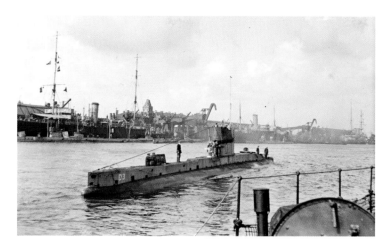

HMS *D3*, shown here after 1914, was lost with all hands in 1918 when mistakenly bombed by a French airship. (N24290: Laforey Collection)

Given the enormous demands placed upon such embryonic technologies, mechanical failures and human errors were unsurprising further sources of accident, and sometimes catastrophe. Lieutenant-Commander Hew Stoker recorded the sudden loss of diving controls that ultimately led to the loss of the Australian submarine HMAS *AE2* in 1915. 'Down and

Off-duty Royal Naval submariners mending clothes and reading, by Francis Dodd, 1918. (Imperial War Museum, ART 918)

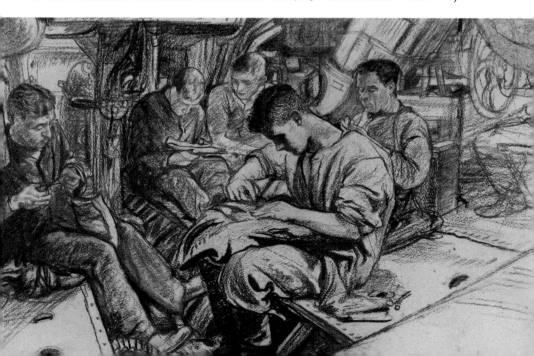

A British
submarine
resting on
the seabed,
watercolour by
W. L. Wyllie,
c. 1917.
(PAF1786)

down and down she went', he wrote, '60, 80, and 100 feet … she seemed to be trying to stand on her nose. Eggs, bread, food of all sorts, knives, forks, plates, came tumbling forward from the petty officers' mess. Everything that could fall over fell; men slipping and struggling.' The large, steam-powered K-class boats proved especially hazardous. The eighteen vessels completed were involved in sixteen major accidents; three were lost in collisions, one disappeared, one sank in harbour and another during its trials. The latter, *K13*, trapped eighty crew members and civilian contractors on the floor of the Gareloch in Scotland. Commander Kenneth Michell remembered how bottles of hot tea and cocoa were passed down to them through an armoured hose, until 'this unfortunately came to a full stop as a soda water bottle got jammed inside'. After fifty-seven hours, the vessel's bows were raised to the surface but thirty-two men had died.

Amid such challenges, it seems extraordinary that crews were able to perform their duties under the additional strains of conflict. And yet the first years of the war saw a number of remarkable achievements. In December 1914, HMS *B11* – commanded by Lieutenant Norman Holbrook – entered the Dardanelles and sank the Ottoman warship *Mesudiye*, earning Holbrook the first Victoria Cross ever awarded to a submariner. In sharp contrast to the reverses suffered by Allied forces ashore in this theatre, HMS *E14* and *E11* inflicted severe losses on Ottoman shipping in 1915, sinking troopships, bombarding shore positions and even landing sailors to demolish railway lines. In the process, they contended with a variety of hazards, including mines, anti-submarine nets and grappling hooks. Famously, *E11* concluded one mission with a live mine snagged on its port hydroplane: it was carried there for more than two hours before it could be detached.

Further north, British submarines entered the Baltic and disrupted the crucial shipments of iron ore from Sweden to Germany. It was there, on 23 October 1915, that *E8* torpedoed and sank the German heavy cruiser *Prinz Adalbert*. The commanding officer, Francis Goodhart, described the scene as follows:

> There was a terrific crash, I looked at the ship, and all that there was, was an immense cloud of thick smoke, she had gone off in one act!! A Mark VIII [torpedo] is some stuff, but it must have got her forward magazine. A marvellous sight and terrifically impressive, bits of the ship were splashing in the water fully 500 yds astern of her … The crew were very bucked and clapped!! I hardly realised I had 'blown up' a ship. Poor devils in her, they can't have known anything about it.

In the Baltic, the North Sea and elsewhere, endless and intermittently nerve-jangling submarine patrols continued until the end of the war. As the Royal Navy's own losses mounted, the ordeal suffered by the families of submariners – who often lived in or close to their bases – must also have been terrible. They are recorded lining the quayside,

> gazing out to the eastward when one of the boats was overdue. The women would stand there for hours, outwardly calm, dry-eyed, but suffering the agony of doubt and uncertainty, hoping against hope that some accident or some defective machinery had caused the delay, but feeling in their hearts that their boat had sailed to the port of missing ships.

THE BATTLE OF JUTLAND
AND BEYOND: 1916–18

Iₙ ₜₕₑ ₚₑ𝐜ₐₚₑₛ...

I N THE DECADES before 1914, British schoolchildren were left in no doubt about the Royal Navy's centrality to their national story. From the defeat of the Spanish Armada in 1588 to the Battle of Trafalgar in 1805, they learned that great sea battles and a line of heroic admirals had propelled Britain to greatness. As a result, the war began with widespread public anticipation that this new conflict would be met – as in the past – with a dramatic naval resolution. The absence of a decisive contest with the German High Seas Fleet in the early years of the war gradually undermined the Navy's immense – but less newsworthy – achievements. For its personnel, spiralling casualty lists from the Western Front brought a haunting sense of under-performance in this hour of need. Based at Scapa Flow, home to the Grand Fleet, Sub-Lieutenant Bowyer-Smyth noted that,

> We live for two things and two things only, our scrap on the Day … and a sight of some of the gentler sex. They don't even give us the illustrated papers now – they're full of this infernal war which we hear such a lot about and see so little of. Upon my soul it is a bit hard – we are supposed to be England's first line of defence and senior service, [but] haven't so much as seen a German.

In May 1916, that 'Day' finally came at the Battle of Jutland, when 250 warships clashed in one of the largest naval

Group of sailors on board the coastal patrol and anti-submarine craft *P59*, 1917–18. (N21754)

actions in history. The result, however, was not the nation's fantasy of Nelsonian annihilation, and the forces of popular expectation were even harder to control in its aftermath than they had been before.

The months before Jutland saw a variety of raids and ruses designed by both sides to draw naval forces from their protected bases. On 31 May, Admiral Reinhard Scheer, commander-in-chief of the High Seas Fleet, took his ships into the North Sea on just such a mission. He planned to use his fast battle-cruisers to bombard the English coast, believing that Admiral Beatty's powerful squadron of battle-cruisers would put to sea in response and could be lured under his guns. In the event, the Admiralty intercepted German communications, and on 30 May not only Beatty's ships but the entire British Grand Fleet were ordered to raise steam. Royal Marine S. J. Salmon, on board HMS *Duke of Edinburgh*, had seen it all before and thought 'it was the usual scare, caused by some of the German ships leaving harbour.' Perhaps with the benefit of hindsight, though, Midshipman John Croome of HMS *Indomitable* remembered that 'everybody seemed to have a premonition that the day had really arrived. There was an almost electric atmosphere.' Watching the clouds of dense, black smoke sent

Admiral Beatty's flagship, HMS *Lion*, leading his battle-cruiser force at the Battle of Jutland, etching with watercolour by W. L. Wyllie, c. 1916. (PAF2246)

up by ship after ship he recalled being 'proudly conscious that I was part of this huge machine and firmly convinced that the machine was invincible, if not even invulnerable.'

The reality was very different. Fighting began at 3.48 p.m. on 31 May when Beatty's battle-cruisers encountered their opposite numbers commanded by Admiral Franz von Hipper. The relatively light deck armour of the British warships left them vulnerable to plunging shells and, within approximately twenty minutes two of them – HMS *Indefatigable* and *Queen Mary* – had blown up at the cost of 2,283 lives. Watching *Indefatigable*'s fate from a nearby destroyer, Sub-Lieutenant Edward Cordeaux 'could clearly see huge funnels, turrets etc. flying through the air, while the column of flame and smoke must have been at least 1,500 feet high.' With the results of German gunnery so evident around him, Midshipman R. M. Dick in the battleship *Barham* understandably remarked that 'for sheer unpleasantness there can be little to beat those seconds which elapse between the flash of the enemy's guns and the fall of the shot – it is an eternity.'

In spite of these losses, Beatty succeeded in drawing Hipper's ships, and the approaching High Seas Fleet, northwards towards the main British force commanded by

These binoculars were recovered by a fishing vessel from the wreckage of the battle-cruiser *Invincible*, which blew up at the Battle of Jutland. (REL0276)

A full-hull model (*c.* 1912) of the battle-cruiser *Queen Mary*, which was destroyed at the Battle of Jutland, 1916. (SLR1408)

Sailors taking on board ammunition for the main armament of the battle-cruiser *Tiger*, 1914–18. (N20359)

The forward fifteen-inch guns of the battleship *Queen Elizabeth* being fired during a training exercise, 1915–16. (N16619: Howe Collection)

Admiral John Jellicoe. This second phase of the battle began at about 6.30 p.m. and brought the massed naval artillery of both nations to bear. Thousands of heavy projectiles, each weighing the best part of a ton, arced towards their targets over miles of water. On board the British battleships, their accuracy was determined by transmitting stations located

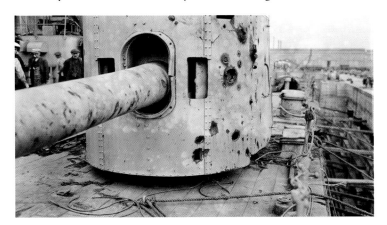

Two photographs showing damage to the battleship *Warspite*, caused by German shells at the Battle of Jutland, 1916. (N16494 and N16489: Howe Collection)

far beneath the waterline. Here, specialised staff operated advanced mechanical computers that processed information from the range-finding equipment and gunnery-control stations above, before delivering new firing solutions to the crews in the turrets. The deck beneath their feet shook with every salvo, and choking dust and cordite smoke billowed from the voice-pipes that communicated their instructions. Nightfall, however, brought an end to long-range gunnery. The battle shifted into a sequence of confused and localised clashes, and under the cover of darkness Admiral Scheer led his fleet back to their bases.

When dawn broke on 1 June, it was clear that the Battle of Jutland was not the clear victory that so many had believed inevitable. While the Royal Navy's command of the seas had not been challenged or even significantly disrupted, it had lost more ships and the list of its dead was more than double that incurred by Germany. The Admiralty's inept handling of the press compounded this ambiguous outcome and sailors sometimes encountered hostility when they returned home. In the words of Midshipman Bill Fell: 'as we passed up the Firth of Forth ... [people] shouted "Cowards! Cowards, you ran away!" and chucked lumps of coal at us. We were received at Rosyth with very, very great disapproval by the local people. They were all in mourning black hats and black arm-bands.' The consequences of the battle for the bodies of those injured were less ambiguous. Shipboard surgeons struggled, in particular, to treat frequently fatal 'flash' burns caused by exploding shells, that caused the skin and epidermis of exposed areas to peel away in sheets. After standing and working continuously for two days and nights, Surgeon-Lieutenant Duncan Lorimer collapsed to the deck, his legs and ankles

This cigarette case (c. 1915–16) was presented to an officer from HMS *Warrior* to commemorate the loss of that ship at the Battle of Jutland. (OBJ0247)

swollen from the effort. He had earlier asked one of the officers' servants

> to leave a double whisky behind the flowerpot in the wardroom. I could not walk and had to go the length of the ship on my hands and knees … I got to the wardroom, collected the whisky, sank into a chair and lighted a cigarette. The next thing I remember was getting shaken up by some attendant … the whisky was un-drunk, the cigarette had burnt to my fingers.

Within the Navy, the legacy of Jutland was also felt far beyond the crews who took part. Unable to sweep Britain's dreadnoughts from the North Sea, Germany became increasingly dependent on a different strategy and a different weapon: the U-boat. By 1916, the

Victoria Cross awarded to Ronald Stuart for his role in the destruction of a German submarine while lieutenant on board the 'Q-ship', HMS *Pargust*, in 1917. (MED1255)

Royal Navy already had considerable experience in countering this threat. Thousands of small vessels, such as trawlers and drifters, had been pressed into service as anti-submarine craft, and devices such as the depth charge – a container the size of an oil drum packed with explosives that could be set to explode beneath the surface – had been successfully deployed. The final years of the conflict also saw the construction of vast minefields designed to deny U-boats access to key sea lanes. On board a patrol craft in 1917, one officer recalled that 'We spent our nights sitting over the tops of minefields with hundreds of trawlers milling around us. Every few minutes a 3,000,000 candle-power flare would be set off. Because of the mines U-boats had to come up and it was hoped they would be illuminated and then hunted by us.' In addition, vessels were developed by the Admiralty to mimic defenceless merchantmen. Known as 'Q-ships' (from their main base at Queenstown, now Cobh, in southern Ireland), their hazardous mission was to lure U-boats to the surface, at

Portrait photograph of Katharine Furse, first director of the Women's Royal Naval Service, c. 1917–18. (A8668/A)

which point concealed guns opened fire and the predator became prey.

However, the appalling losses of cargo vessels in early 1917 – totalling almost 900,000 tons in April alone – revealed the desperate need for more effective measures. After protracted consideration, a system of convoys guarded by warships was introduced, leading to a marked reduction in sinkings. The Navy might have entered the conflict anticipating a titanic clash of battlefleets, but it was through the unglamorous and generally uneventful toil of these convoy escorts that one of its greatest contributions to victory was made. It is, perhaps, inevitable that the blizzard of diary and letter writing memorialising Jutland was not similarly spurred by these more routine but no less significant endeavours. The vast manpower requirements occasioned by the Navy's ever-expanding fleet and myriad responsibilities did, though, have an outcome that claimed widespread attention. In 1917, Katharine Furse – previously a leading light of the Voluntary Aid Detachment – was appointed first director of the Women's Royal Naval Service. Numbering five-thousand ratings and almost five hundred officers by the end of the war, the 'Wrens', as they came to be known, did vital work as clerks, typists, wireless telegraphists, electricians, cooks and drivers.

With its occasional crescendos of success or horror, the anti-submarine campaign wore on until Armistice Day in November 1918. One of its more bizarre incidents was recorded by Ordinary Seaman Stan Smith. Spotting something resembling a submarine, his ship went full ahead to ram it. 'We hit the vessel', he wrote, just as what appeared to be the bow lifted from a large swell. We immediately wished we hadn't as the contents of the thing shot all over the ship, showering us as far aft as the funnel, and oh boy! What a stink! It turned out to be a huge bloated dead whale … Goodness knows how long it had been floating around for it was white with seagull droppings.

Amid these shifting operational priorities, the Royal Navy was never given an opportunity to re-fight Jutland and to exorcise its ghosts with outright triumph. The final major naval actions of the war occurred in April 1918 with raids against the Belgian ports of Zeebrugge and Ostend, important U-boat bases. Pressed home with extraordinary and costly heroism against German coastal defences, the attacks nevertheless failed in their ambition to close these ports to German shipping. But with the grim irony so indicative of the conflict as a whole, its survivors reached England to find the press erupting with tales of glorious victory.

The capstan top from the cruiser *Vindictive* (1897), which took part in raids on both Zeebrugge and Ostend in 1918. (REL0458)

Study showing a Royal Marine carrying a Lewis gun during the raid on Zeebrugge in 1918, watercolour by W. L. Wyllie, c. 1930. (PAD9948)

CONCLUSION

Wʜᴇɴ ᴛʜᴇ ᴇɴᴅ finally came, it was accompanied by crushing symbolism. On 21 November 1918, ten days after the Armistice had been signed, seventy vessels from the German High Seas Fleet were escorted across the North Sea by approximately 370 British and Allied warships. Admiral Beatty, now commander-in-chief of the Grand Fleet, watched from the bridge of his flagship, HMS *Queen Elizabeth*, as they arrived in the Firth of Forth for subsequent internment at Scapa Flow, Orkney. The following day, parties of Royal Naval officers went on board, and came face to face with

their adversaries. Years of bitter conflict left them brimming with suspicion and mistrust. Beneath the waterline in the battle-cruiser SMS *Hindenburg*, Lieutenant-Commander C. A. Colville was caught momentarily off guard:

> While we were looking round an order was given in German and there was immediately a loud hissing of compressed air. We most of us thought that our last moment had arrived, and that they were going to play some dirty trick, having got the admiral and a good bag of officers down below, but we were comforted by the knowledge that if we were done in, at least the Huns down there would also perish with us.

At the end of that month, the German ships were moved to Scapa Flow where, on 21 June 1919, in a secretly concerted plan, most were scuttled by their crews to prevent their division among the victorious allies.

The conclusion of the war did not eradicate all of its random horrors. An unnamed sailor coming back from the

HMS *Cardiff* leading the German High Seas Fleet to internment in the Firth of Forth, oil on canvas by Charles Dixon, 1919. (BHC0670)

Mediterranean recorded the following ghastly vignette on 17 November 1918:

> Last week an American oil tanker caught fire here. One man tried to escape thro' a port, and was jammed half way. A rope was put round him but all efforts to shift him proved unsuccessful. He begged them to shoot him, the fire burning his legs inside and the heat intense. A fitter from the dockyard offered to cut him out with a blow lamp, but was not allowed as an explosion was expected. A doctor then gave him … [a lethal] injection and he died.

A bass drum from the band of the battle-cruiser *Lion*, painted with the ship's battle honours from Heligoland Bight, Dogger Bank and Jutland, 1916–24. (AAB0231)

Moreover, large numbers of Royal Naval personnel continued to fight Bolshevik Russian forces in the Baltic and the Black Sea. After years of bloody struggle against Germany, the reality of further casualties on this forgotten front – in combination with growing protests at naval pay and living conditions – led to instances of unrest and mutiny. For the majority of sailors, though, their active service had finished. While often unseen and unreported, the contribution they had made was immense. From operations spanning the globe in 1914, the Royal Navy had gradually concentrated the maritime war in European waters. Without its protection of trade and troop transportation, its blockade of German ports and its multifaceted response to Germany's naval threat, Britain's war effort would have unravelled. No amount of courage and sacrifice in the fighting on land would have altered this outcome.

SUGGESTED READING

THIS BOOK DRAWS on the archival resources of the Caird Library at the National Maritime Museum, including the following collections of personal papers: Anonymous sailor (JOD/198); Baker, Stephen (JOD/149); Bennett, Harry (JOD/106/1); Blood, M. (JOD/164/1); Burrow, E. (REC/24); Colson, Bernard (MSS/74/177); Dannreuther, Hubert (DAN/516, 547–8); Dent, Ronald (MSS/87/059); Dick, Royer (DCK/5); Edwards, Kenneth (MSS/74/113); Enstone, Albert (MSS/72/094); Findlay, Jack (JOD/253); Giffard, Frederick (AGC/4/38); Gipps, G. (JOD/117); Hanson, Percy (MSS/81/042.1); Jukes-Hughes, Edward (JHS/3); Kneale, Alfred (JOD/131); Oliver, Robert (OLI/37); Pawley, Sylvester (DAN/454); Phillips, E. (JOD/204); Salmon, S. (JOD/244); Whittaker, Jack (WHR/2); Wood, Henry (TRN/74); Woodland, Clement (JOD/107)

First-person testimonies of the war quoted here have also been sourced from some of the following volumes, all of which are highly recommended as further reading:

Arthur, Max. *Lost Voices of the Royal Navy*. Hodder, 2005.

Benbow, Tim. *British Naval Aviation: The First 100 Years*. Ashgate, 2011.

Bennett, Geoffrey. *The Battle of Jutland*. Pen & Sword, 2006.

Everitt, Don. *K Boats: Steam-powered Submarines in World War I*. US Naval Institute Press, 1999.

Halpern, Paul G. *A Naval History of World War I*. UCL Press, 1994.

Jerrold, Douglas. *The Royal Naval Division*. Hutchinson, 1923.

Kemp, Paul. *British Submarines of World War One*. Weidenfeld Military, 1990.

Lambert, Nicholas (ed.) *The Submarine Service, 1900–18.* Ashgate, 2001.

Lavery, Brian. *Able Seamen: The Lower Deck of the Royal Navy, 1850–1939.* Conway, 2011.

Liddle, Peter. *The Sailor's War, 1914–18.* Blandford, 1985.

Mackay, Richard. *A Precarious Existence: British Submarines in World War One.* Periscope Publishing, 2003.

Perrett, Bryan. *North Sea Battleground: The War at Sea, 1914–18.* Pen & Sword, 2011.

Philpott, Maryam. *Air and Sea Power in World War I: Combat and Experience in the Royal Flying Corps and the Royal Navy.* IB Tauris, 2012.

Redford, Duncan. *The Submarine: A Cultural History from the Great War to Nuclear Combat.* IB Tauris, 2010.

Rosher, Harold. *In the Royal Naval Air Service: Being the War Letters of the Late Harold Rosher to his Family.* Chatto & Windus, 1916.

Sellers, Leonard. *The Hood Battalion: Royal Naval Division: Antwerp, Gallipoli, France, 1914–1918.* Leo Cooper, 1995.

Sparrow, Geoffrey. *On Four Fronts with the Royal Naval Division.* Hodder & Stoughton, 1918.

Steel, Nigel and Hart, Peter. *Jutland 1916: Death in the Grey Wastes.* Cassell, 2004.

Thompson, Julian. *The Imperial War Museum Book of the War at Sea, 1914–1918.* Sidgwick & Jackson, 2005.

Wilson, Michael. *Destination Dardanelles: The Story of HMS E7.* Pen & Sword, 1988.

Winton, John. *Submariners: Life in British Submarines, 1901–1999.* Constable & Robinson, 2001.

PLACES TO VISIT

Aberdeen Maritime Museum, Shiprow, Aberdeen, AB11 5BY.
   Telephone: 01224 337700. Website: www.aagm.co.uk/
   Venues/AberdeenMaritimeMuseum

Explosion! The Museum of Naval Firepower, Heritage
   Way, Priddy's Hard, Gosport, Hampshire PO12 4LE.
   Telephone: 023 9250 5600. Website: www.explosion.org.uk

Fleet Air Arm Museum, RNAS Yeovilton, Ilchester, Somerset
   BA22 8HT. Telephone: 01935 840565.
   Website: www.fleetairarm.com

HMS Belfast, The Queen's Walk, London SE1 2JH.
   Telephone: 020 7940 6300.
   Website: www.iwm.org.uk/visits/hms-belfast

Imperial War Museum, Lambeth Road, London SE1 6HZ.
   Telephone: 020 7416 5000.
   Website: www.iwm.org.uk/visits/iwm-london

Imperial War Museum North, The Quays, Trafford Wharf Road,
   Manchester M17 1TZ. Telephone: 0161 836 4012.
   Website: www.iwm.org.uk/visits/iwm-north

Merseyside Maritime Museum, Albert Dock, Liverpool
   Waterfront, Liverpool L3 4AQ. Telephone: 0151 478 4499.
   Website: www.liverpoolmuseums.org.uk/maritime

National Maritime Museum, Park Row, Greenwich,
   London SE10 9NF. Telephone: 020 8312 6608.
   Website: www.rmg.co.uk

Royal Naval Museum, HM Naval Base, Portsmouth,
   Hampshire PO1 3NH. Telephone: 023 9272 7562.
   Website: www.royalnavalmuseum.org

The Royal Navy Submarine Museum, Haslar Jetty Road,
   Gosport, Hampshire PO12 2AS. Telephone: 023 9251
   0354. Website: www.submarine-museum.co.uk

Scapa Flow Visitor Centre and Museum, Lyness, Hoy, Orkney.
   Telephone: 01856 791300. Website: www.scapaflow.co.uk
   (Seasonal: museum closed during the winter.)

INDEX